# Finding O :
# The Great
# Alphabet Hunt

## Paula Curtis Taylorson

illustrated by Caterina Cozza

Finding O : The Great Alphabet Hunt

This is a work of fiction.

Text and Illustrations copyrighted

by Paula Curtis Taylorson ©2021

Library of Congress Control Number: 2021905039



Printed in the United States of America

A 2 Z Press LLC

PO Box 582

Deleon Springs, FL 32130

bestlittleonlinebookstore.com

sizemore3630@aol.com

440-241-3126

ISBN: 978-1-954191-16-7

# Dedication

*Thank you to those
who read to me and
those who listened
to me read.*

# This book belongs to:

_____________________________

It's **Olympic** time in **old** ancient Greece.

ORIGAMI

Our **outstanding** athletes have begun,
**Obsessively** looking **out** for
all the **O** words..
It's both **outrageous** and **obvious** fun!

Oscar, an assistant **official**,
is helped by **Ophelia**, his **obstinate** pet.

**Ophelia's** an **orphan Oregon Rex**
cat with an attitude.
She's so **obnoxious** she won't
move 'til she's had her **omelet**.

The **oven** is hot, and the **olive oil** is ready.
'Come **on or** we'll be late
for the **opening** games.'
The **okra** are diced
and the **oregano's** sliced,
Oh, **Ophelia**, won't miss the
torch of the flames!

OLIVE
OIL

The first event to **observe** is an **obstacle** sprint.
**Overtly**, an **orangutan** fumbles **over** an **ox**.

Followed by an **otter** called **Owen**,
And an **orange octogenarian** fox.

Next, is the **original off-road** running race.
Some **obliging oysters** are leading the way.

An **ostrich** runs in the **opposite** direction
Ignoring the **oval** sign this road is : '**One** Way!'

ONE WAY !
OSTRI

**Outside** the stadium, down at the **ocean,**
The swimmers are **orderly** and **obey** the rule.

'No **obstructing** each **other or** splashing around,'
says the **officer** who's an **outspoken** mule!

OFFSHORE

Orange Eating Cont

An **obedient Old** English Sheepdog
eats **oranges** with juice that is **oozing**.

While an **octopus** tries to high jump a pole,
but his eight feet make it **oddly** confusing!

**Overhead,** an **osprey** has a video camera,
The **ornithologists** look up at the **ominous** clouds.

He's filming the **orienteering,**
But it's going to rain **on** the **oblivious** crowds.

OVERCAST
START

In the sand pit they're digging for **opals**.
We hear **ooing** and **ouching** and **oinking out** loud.

An **ogre** is in the **octagonal** hole,
making **onomatopoeia** noises
for the **onlooking** crowd.

The **optimistic** winner **of** the marathon,
Openly **outshines** the **others**
with an **overwhelming** lead.

**Overjoyed** at his **Olympian** effort,
the **Oryx** ran 26 miles at **optimum** speed.

Then OMG! Something strange is occurring,
at the opposing end of the tracks.

Four little ocelots are doing a relay,
with oxygen tanks on their backs.

OUTSTANDING

The **orchestra** strikes up an anthem **okay**,
But the **oboe** is way **out of** tune.

And, an **optician** from **Oslo** in **overalls**,
plays the **organ** with an **ordinary** spoon.

OFF-KEY

An **oriental opossum** shot put an **overarm** throw, sending an **onion obscurely** in an **outward** direction.

The **orb** skimmed the head of an **outlandish orca** and plopped in **ointment** in the first-aiders' section.

At **once**, Oscar **objected** to the **ornery owl** who was
**Occupied** in painting **omicrons onto** the wall.

But his **once-off** graffiti turned
**out** to be the **Olympic** rings,
An **occasion** which was celebrated by all.

This time we **outwitted** the O words,
This capital letter has
been **outgrown** and versed.

**Often,** the words just fly **out of** the book,
But there's **other** letters to **overcome** first!

# The End

# My Very Own 'O' Words:

# Glossary

**Page 1. Olympic** : the greatest of the games or festivals of ancient Greece, held every four years in the plain of Olympia in Elis, in honor of Zeus.
**Old** :  far advanced in the years of one's or its life or creation

**Page 3. Our** : belonging to someone
**Outstanding** : marked by superiority or distinction, Excellent, distinguished
**Obsessively** : to think about something unceasingly or persistently, dwell upon something
Looking **out** for : the act of searching for something
**O** : a letter
**Outrageous** :  highly unusual or unconventional, extravagant;, remarkable
**Obvious** : easily seen, recognized, or understood, open to view or knowledge, evident

**Page 4. Oscar** : a boy or man's name
**Official** : a person appointed or elected to a position or charged with certain duties
**Ophelia** : a girl or woman's name
**Obstinate** : stubborn, unwilling to co-operate
Also on Page 4 : **Octopus** : a sea creature with a large head and many legs

**Page 5. Orphan** : a little one without parents
**Oregon Rex cat** : a special breed of hairless cats
**Obnoxious** : mischievous, acting badly at times
**Omelet** : a food made with eggs, cheese, and vegetables

**Page 6. Oven** : a chamber or compartment, as in a stove, for baking, roasting, heating, drying,
**Olive Oil** : oil made from olives, used in cooking and food

Page 6 (continued). **On** : so as to be or remain supported by or suspended from, taking place, occurring
**Or** : used to connect words, comparing
**Opening** : the beginning of the games here
**Okra** : a vegetable, food
**Oregano** : a spice used in food flavoring
**Oh** : used in direct address to attract the attention of the person spoken to

Page 8. **Observe** : to look at closely
**Obstacle** : something that obstructs or hinders progress
overtly open to view or knowledge; not concealed or secret
**Overtly** : something that is easily seen or noticed
**Orangutan** : a large monkey that is orange/red colored
**Over** : above in place or position, higher up
**Ox** : a large animal similar to a cow

Page 9. **Otter** : an animal in the weasel family
**Owen** : a boy or man's name
**Orange** : a color
**Octogenarian** : between the ages of 80-90
Also on page 9 : **Okapi** : a large animal that looks like a cross between a deer and a zebra

Page 10. **Original** : something that is new, fresh, inventive, novel
**Off-road** : a race not on a usual track, it is off the road ways
**Obliging** : someone or something consenting or agreeing to do something
**Oysters** : a marine mollusk that live in a shell
**Ostrich** : a large, two footed, flightless bird
**Opposite** : different, not the same, radically different in some respect common to both, as in nature, qualities, direction, result, or significance

Page 10.  (Continued). **Oval** :  having the general form, shape, or outline of an egg; egg-shaped.
**One-way** :  being or amounting to a single direction

Page 12. **Outside** :  being, acting, or doing something beyond a boundary or enclosure, not inside
**Ocean** : the vast body of salt water that covers almost three fourths of the earth's surface.
**Orderly** : arranged or disposed in a neat, tidy manner or in a regular sequence
**Obey** : to comply with or follow the commands, restrictions, wishes, or instructions of

Page 13. **Obstructing**  : block someone from doing something,  hinder
**Other** : different, distinct, additional or further
**Officer** : a person who holds a position of rank or authority in the army, navy, air force, or any similar organization, one who holds a commission. a member of a police department or a constable.
**Outspoken** : free or unreserved in speech

Page 14. **Obedient** : doing the right thing, comply with rules
**OLD English Sheepdog** : a dog with long, shaggy hair
**Oranges** :  fruit
**Oozing** :  to flow, percolate, or exude slowly, as through holes or small

Page 15. **Octopus** : a sea creature with many legs
**Oddly** : differing in nature from what is ordinary, usual, or expected fantastic; bizarre

Page 16. **Overhead** :  in the air
**Osprey** : a large bird resembling a hawk
**Ornithologist** : the branch of zoology that deals with birds
**Ominous** : portending evil or harm; foreboding; threatening

Page 17. **Organized** :  to form as or into a whole
consisting of interdependent or coordinated parts,
especially for united action - orderly
**Orienteering** : a sport of treasure hunting with map reading
and check points, participants go where they are not familiar
with and they use only a compass and a map to find their way
**Oblivious** : unmindful; unconscious; unaware

Page 18. **Opals** : a gem, jewelry of different colors
and sometimes milky white with blue or green mixed in
**Ooing** : a word that sounds like it spells
**Ouching** : a word that sounds like it spells
**Oinking** : a word that sounds like it spells
**Out loud** : so it can be heard

Page 19. **Out-going** : Some with energy to do things
**Ogre** : a monster in fairy tales usually represented
as a hideous giant who feeds on human
**Octagonal** : a figure with eight sides
**Onomatopoeias** : the formation of a word, as *cuckoo*,
*meow*, *honk*, or *boom*, by imitation of a sound made
by or associated with its referent
**On-lookers** : people standing around watching the events

Page 20. **Optimistic** : one who takes a favorable view of
events or conditions and expects the most
favorable outcome
**Openly** : something done so it is easily seen or viewed
**Outshine** : surpassing the others' efforts
**Others** : the ones competing also
**Overwhelming** : very much more effort than the others

Page 21. **Overjoyed** : exuberant happiness, very happy
**Olympic record** : the measurement of the effort in the specific event at the Olympic competition
**Oryx** : a large animal resembling a deer
**Optimum** : the best or most favorable result obtained

Page 22. **OMG** : slang for 'Oh, my God'
**Occurring** : something happening
**Opposing** : not the same side, other side

Page 23. **Ocelots** : a wild cat with spots
**Oxygen** : a gas in the air that mammals breath

Page 24. **Orchestra** : a group of performers on various musical instruments
**Okay** :  something that is alright, correct, permissible
**Oboe** : a woodwind musical instrument
**Out of tune** : not making the correct sounds

Page 25. **Optician** : a person who makes and sells eyeglasses
**Oslo** : a sea port in Norway
**Overalls** :  clothing that is worn over other garments
**Organ** : a large musical instrument similar to a piano
**Ordinary** :  of no special quality or interest

Page 26. **Oriental** : something or someone from the orient, the countries in Asia
**Overarm** : a motion of throwing over the shoulder
**Onion** : a vegetable, food
**Obscurely** : not clear or plain to understand; uncertain:
**Outward** : to go in a motion away from the original place
**Orb** : a sphere, globe, circular object
**Outlandish** : bizarre, odd or strange behavior

Page 26. (continued) : **Orca** : a black and white whale
Also on page 26. **Opossum** :  a small animal  that carries
its babies in a pouch

Page 27. **Ointment** :  a soft substance with medicine
to apply to the skin

Page 28. **Objected** : to offer a reason or argument in
opposition. to express or feel disapproval or dislike
**Ornery** : mischievous, bad behavior
**Owl** :  a bird that comes out at night time with a
large wing span and silent flight
**Occupied** : to give one's attention to, engage in
**Omicrons** : a letter of the Greek alphabet **the fifteenth letter of the
Greek alphabet (O, o), transliterated as 'o.'**
**Onto** : to put something to the surface of something else

Page 29. **Once** off : unique, one of a kind
**Olympic rings** : the 5 colored rings symbol of the Olympic games
**Occasion** :  a particular time of a special event to
celebrate or accomplish

Page 30. **Outwitted** : to get the better of by superior
ingenuity or cleverness .

Page 31. **Outgrown** : to grow too large for, to leave
behind or lose in the changes incident to development
or the passage of time

Page 32. **Often** : many times; frequently
**Out of** : from among something, from a source
**Overcome** :  to get the better of in a struggle or
conflict; conquer, defeat, to prevail over, surmount
**Other** : additional or further: different or distinct
from the one or ones already mentioned or implied
**Off** : so as to be no longer supported or attached

Paula  Curtis-Taylorson  Lives  in  Marston  Mortaine England. She is a full-time secondary school teacher of English and English Literature. She was amongst the first of the initial students to graduate from the Uk's first BA (Hons) Creative Writing Program at the University of Bedfordshire.

Her first love is poetry and rhyme and she works hard to inspire and teach appreciation of the subject to all age groups. Many of her students have gone on to be successful writers.